All things considered

The Toronto Blessing &
Real Christianity

by Tony Payne

St Matthias Press
Sydney • London • Capetown

All things considered
© St Matthias Press, 1995
(Originally published in Australia as 'No laughing matter')

St Matthias Press
PO Box 665
LONDON SW20 8RU
ENGLAND
Tel: (0181) 947 5658 Fax: (0181) 944 7091

Scripture taken from the HOLY BIBLE, NEW INTERNA-
TIONAL VERSION. Copyright © 1973, 1978, 1984 Interna-
tional Bible Society. Used by permission of Zondervan Publishers.

ISBN 1-873166-15-X

Contents

Introduction

WHEN A NEW TREND or movement emerges within Christianity, it is often difficult to know how to react. We don't want to leap to the battlements, boiling oil at the ready, at the sound of every new voice or suggestion. Yet, we also do not want to lower our draw-bridge every time there is a knock at the door. The Scriptures warn us to be on the lookout for false teachers and distractions to the gospel. We need to be on our guard, and not uncritically accept every new thing that comes along.

Sometimes, it can be difficult to distinguish the helpful new approach from the dangerous distraction. Even those new movements which are dangerous don't always appear that way at first sight. They usually have enough truth and attractiveness mixed up with them to be appealing. It sometimes takes time to assess whether a new movement is heading in the right direction.

This booklet traces my own developing reactions to one such new movement, the movement that has become popularly known as the Toronto Blessing. I start by recording encounters with two streams of the Toronto movement, those associated with Rodney Howard-Browne and with the Toronto Airport Vineyard Church itself in Canada.

The third chapter, however, is the important one. It takes a broader, more considered look at the important questions that the Toronto debate raises about the nature of biblical Christianity. For while there is good reason to believe that the Toronto Blessing, with its various manifestations and characteristics, will pass into history like so many other movements of its type, the questions that it raises will not—questions about how we know and relate to God, how we conduct our Christian lives and ministries, what the role of the Holy Spirit is, and so on.

These questions will remain with us for some time. They will be posed to us anew by the next Toronto-style movement that comes along. We need to get back to the apostolic testimony in the Scriptures and be clear in our minds on these fundamental issues. Otherwise we might find ourselves falling under the same rebuke that Paul issued to the Corinthians in 2 Corinthians 11:3-4 (see margin).

May this not be said of us.

But I am afraid that just as Eve was deceived by the serpent's cunning, your minds may somehow be led astray from your sincere and pure devotion to Christ. For if someone comes to you and preaches a Jesus other than the Jesus we preached, or if you receive a different spirit from the one you received, or a different gospel from the one you accepted, you put up with it easily enough. (2 Cor 11:3-4).

If you're new to Christianity...

You might be reading this booklet as someone who hasn't had very much to do with Christianity up till now. You might have friends or relatives involved in the Toronto Blessing; or you might simply be curious about what is going on.

The material in this booklet was written for Christians who were confused or concerned about the Toronto Blessing. It therefore contains some in-house Christian jargon, biblical references and theological language that you might find a bit hard to follow in a few places (although I've tried to simplify where possible). All the same, the gist of the argument should be straightforward.

If, after finishing this booklet, you have any questions, or would like to find out more about Jesus and what he taught, please write to me via the publishers. I'd be happy to supply you with some more information.

Tony Payne
September 1995

Rodney Howard-Browne is one of the key figures in what has become known as 'the Toronto Blessing'. His controversial style, his close association with fringe pentecostal leaders like Kenneth Copeland and Kenneth Hagin, and his claims to be God's 'Holy Ghost bartender', have led many to question the legitimacy of his ministry. When he came to town earlier this year to lead a series of rallies, I went along.

1 No Laughing Matter

RODNEY HOWARD-BROWNE walked slowly down the aisle in my direction. He is a bull of a man, short, thick-necked and tremendously broad across the shoulders.

He pointed at the man sitting in front of me, "Dear brother, come here. Stand up and come right here. Raise your hands and close your eyes." The man did as he was told. Mr Howard-Browne stretched out his hand towards the man. "Oh yes, here it comes. Wadeh cuma ho ho shayim (or words to that effect). Right now!" The man collapsed backwards, was caught by some waiting attendants and gently lowered to the floor. I looked at his face. It was calm and smiling, as if he were having a pleasant dream.

What would I do or say if he pointed next at me? Everyone else he had called upon in the last 20 minutes had gone down. Some shook. Some collapsed before they had made it out of their seats. One man swayed towards the floor several times but did not go down, like a punch-drunk boxer trying to make it to the end of the round. Mr Howard-Browne was not interested in a points decision. "Don't fight it. Let go. Hit him again, Jesus. Now!" Down he went. Others were lying on the floor in groups where they had fallen, some laughing, some just smiling, others making groaning noises. One man quite close to me was lying flat on his back laughing uncontrollably, as if being tickled by some invisible agent. Mr Howard-Browne returned to him and with a grin put his shoe on the man's chest. The man grabbed his ankle and laughed all the louder, as did all those around.

Another thought also disturbed me. What if I swoon or go into a trance like the lady down the front on the left? She had stood motionless with eyes closed and arms raised for 30 seconds before going down, and Mr Howard-Browne had taken a camera from someone nearby and taken a family snap for her to remember the occasion. What if he did that to me and published the photographs? My credibility would be in tatters.

I looked slowly up from the man lying on the floor beside me. My heart was pounding. It was 1:30 pm. We had been in the meeting since 10, and I had not eaten since breakfast. It was hot. I felt slightly giddy and light-headed. Despite my intentions otherwise, I feared that if I was called upon to stand up, close my eyes and raise my hands I too would be a goner.

I frantically tried to think what I would say. A strong "No thank you" perhaps? Or "No, I'm feeling rather tired. You sit down here if you want to talk to me." Rodney Howard-Browne looked at me, and then turned slowly and headed back down the aisle. For the first and only time that morning I said quiet prayer of gratitude: 'Thank you Lord.'

THIS CLOSE ENCOUNTER of the pentecostal kind took place on February 7, 1995 at a meeting organized by the Christian Life Centre at Brookvale in Sydney. The visiting speaker, Rodney Howard-Browne, is a prominent exponent of the 'Toronto blessing', a phenomenon of alleged spiritual revival which has Christians talking in Canada, the US and Britain.

It all started in January of last year in Toronto, Canada, (hence the name) at the Wimber-affiliated Airport Vineyard Church. An outbreak of very demonstrative and widespread physical manifestations (such as falling down, shaking, and in particular uncontrollable laughing) convinced those present that God was giving them a special anointing or time of revival. People flocked to see what was happening and to taste the blessing for themselves. It spread. Evangelists like Rodney Howard-Browne now take the 'blessing' with them to churches all over the world.

As with the John Wimber brouhaha of a few years ago, Bible-believing Christians are being divided over what is happening. In England, the 'blessing' has been greeted with some enthusiasm, one prominent Evangelical Alliance pastor going so far as to say: "I believe we are on the edge of what could be the greatest thing to hit our nation this century".[1] Others are not so sure. The Evangelical Alliance thought it necessary to call a special consultation in December of last year to discuss the phenomenon, and to issue a cautious joint statement about it.

1. Gerald Coates quoted in 'Evangelicals Now', Oct 1994, p. 8.

Is this Toronto Blessing anything new, and what are we to make of it all?

What's new

The meeting opened with a lengthy, expertly led and superbly accompanied singing session. The band was without doubt the best I have heard in a Christian meeting. The songs were musically very good—exciting, fast-moving, and singable—and flowed seamlessly from one to the next, with times of informal worship in tongues happening between some of them. Judging by the faces and bodily attitudes of those around me, the effect of 45 minutes of this, all standing, and most of it with arms raised, was quite intoxicating.

The singing was followed by a 50 minute talk from Rodney Howard-Browne on the importance of financially supporting itinerant evangelists, although he denied repeatedly that he was after money himself. There was some more singing.

So far, nothing new—a common or garden pentecostal meeting.

There followed, however, something that *was* new—a second sermon, lasting nearly an hour, which contained trenchant criticism of a number of pentecostal sacred cows. The practice of daily 'putting the armour on'; the obsession of some churches with 'territorial spirits'; the fascination with casting out demons and putting the angels out over our loved ones and possessions; the importance of all-night prayer as the precursor to revival—all were lambasted by Mr Howard-Browne as part of our ongoing obsession with finding the 'secret' to the anointing. He insisted that there was no formula, no secret, no set of things that one had to 'do' in order to receive the anointing. "The anointing is not a formula; it is a relationship." (*Cheers. Amens.*) If God really was alive, and ready to bless (*more Amens*), then all you had to do was yield to him. You had to relax, not take yourself so seriously, and let the Jesus in your belly come bubbling out. It's up to God. He'll do it. We need to be freed from the bondage of trying to get it to happen by our own techniques. Just let it happen.

All this was cleverly done, with plenty of humour. The sad irony, of course, was that the whole meeting, and particularly the 'ministry time' that followed the sermon, was nothing but another example of this ongoing search for the secret of the 'anointing'. Mr Howard-Browne, and the Toronto Blessing, are nothing else but the newest and best way to be 'touched by the Spirit'.

As the meeting proceeded, and people started being laid out, nothing happened that hasn't been well-documented in pentecostal movements throughout the world during this century. Indeed, John Wimber is quoted in *Christianity Today* as saying that the Toronto manifestations are not particularly new to the Vineyard fellowship: "Nearly everything we've seen—falling, weeping, laughing, shaking—has been seen before, not only in our own memory, but in revivals all over the world"[1]. I certainly saw nothing that I had not seen (and participated in) in charismatic meetings in the late 70s. It was a reprise of good ol' fashioned Holy Ghost revivalism, 90s style. There were the usual techniques— long meetings, plenty of singing, plenty of standing, an engaging speaker who persuaded you to like and trust him, the expectation that things would happen, the suggestion that things would happen, seeing things happen to other people, the standing with eyes closed and arms raised before receiving the 'touch'.

It was all so carefully managed and so artfully staged, that I wondered how anyone could possibly believe that this was a spontaneous activity of the Spirit of God. I wondered how anyone could imagine that there was no 'technique' or method involved (as the sermon protested), and that it was simply an example of God 'doing whatever he wanted to do' (an oft-repeated phrase). Why did the anointing not fall in the middle of the sermon? Or at the very beginning of the meeting? Why did the Spirit not slay the musicians in mid-song, or Rodney himself in mid-gesture? Why did it all happen after three hours of preparation and mediated only through the preacher?

There is unfortunately something else that is not new about the Toronto blessing—and that is that evangelical Christians are being taken in by it.

What are we to make of it?

The quest for the New is one of the abiding characteristics of pentecostal movements everywhere. The very theology of pentecostalism requires that God keep doing new things. Fresh and exciting 'moves of God' must keep occurring, for pentecostalism draws its life from what God is doing now, here, *in me*, rather than on what God has revealed and done, *for me*, in Jesus. This explains the criticism by Howard-Browne of existing pentecostal techniques. The old must be demolished to make way for the new.

If we look back over pentecostalism's recent history, God begins to appear like a good marketing manager. He needs to relaunch his product every few years, with some new packaging and some new improved features—first as the 'Baptism in the Spirit' with tongues, then as 'the healing ministry', then as 'the healing of memories' (remember that?), then as 'power evangelism', then as 'words of knowledge', and now it seems as the Toronto Blessing.

The charismatic or pentecostal alternative is ever-present and ever-changing. It presents itself under new names and guises, and will always do so, for its very nature is to relentlessly pursue the New. Underneath, however, there is nothing new. It is the same theology, mystical in its structures, focusing on us and our experience rather than on God and his work, and distracting us from proclaiming the gospel of Christ crucified.

The new packaging is invariably attractive. Why would we expect it to be otherwise? In the mid-80s, it was John Wimber, coming to us as a self-proclaimed evangelical, promising a new lease of life to tired, rationalistic preachers. Now in the mid-90s, we have an outbreak of physical manifestations which are being marketed under the 'Jonathan Edwards' brand-name. The Toronto evangelists quite explicitly claim that their experience is in a direct line of descent from the revival that broke out in New England under Jonathan Edwards nearly 200 years ago. Again, the message is subtle but clear. "This may look like just another push by pentecostalism, but really it is Jonathan Edwards again in your midst. Jonathan Edwards—great reformed and evangelical theologian. He had strange things happen in his meetings. So do we. We're true blue. Climb aboard."

The Jonathan Edwards connection is distant, to say the least, as those who have read Edwards will know. His theology, methods and emphasis are a world away from the Toronto Blessing.

One question remains however. If we recognize the Toronto Blessing as simply another pentecostal incarnation, what are we to make of the physical manifestations? Is that not a worry? Should we deny that these things are taking place? Are they of God or the Devil? How are we to explain them?

So that we know what we are talking about, let us list the kinds of phenomena involved. When the anointing falls, participants report the following:

- feelings of weightlessness
- feelings of heaviness
- a feeling of being stretched
- catalepsy (being unable to move)
- shaking
- repetitive movement of body parts
- rapid eye movement
- changes in breathing
- tinglings
- alleviation of pain and diseases (such as migraines, stuttering, back pain, dyslexia, bursitis, and so on)
- a feeling that body parts are changing in size or swelling
- a feeling of being detached from your body
- a powerful feeling of energy or electricity coursing through the body
- hearing a buzzing noise

- changes in hearing
- smelling a sweet aroma, like flowers
- seeing a bright light
- being aware of hot and cold areas on the body
- feeling drunk
- feeling washed clean
- a distortion in the awareness of time passing
- age regression (vividly recalling and even acting out child-hood incidents)
- uncontrollable laughter.

Most of these phenomena are being experienced under the Toronto Blessing, and all of them have been reported as regular occurrences in pentecostal meetings when people are 'slain in the Spirit'.[2]

What is really interesting is that all of these phenomena are also well-documented as being the common results of hypnosis.[3] Subjects undergoing mass hypnosis regularly exhibit precisely these manifestations, sometimes by auto-suggestion and sometimes *spontaneously*. Equally interesting is that the conditions that produce such hypnotic phenomena show remarkable similarities to Toronto style meetings—the leadership or control of a central figure, an atmosphere of intensified emotion, a strong motivation and expectation in the participants, and the opportunity to imitate others so affected.

Moreover, apologists for these manifestations of the Spirit readily admit that certain sorts of people seem more susceptible (more 'open to the Spirit') than others. As Francis MacNutt observes in his book *Overcome by the Spirit*:

> People determinedly self-controlled are not nearly so likely to be overcome by the Spirit...people with compressed lips and tight jaws...
>
> I have noticed that artistic, creative, intuitive people seem more likely to fall than rational, intellectual types.... In general, more women than men seem to experience resting ['resting' is one of MacNutt's phrases for falling over or being slain in the Spirit].
>
> The most likely to rest would be a young woman of Latin American or African ancestry, of artistic bent...whose childhood has been filled with games and laughter...

2. For details, see N. Mikhaiel, 'Slaying in the Spirit' (Punchbowl: Bruised Reed, 1992) pp. 16-34.

3. Ibid.

> If I could characterize the kind of person least likely to fall…he would be an elderly man of Anglo-Saxon or Germanic ancestry who had a hard childhood and very little play.[4]

4. F. MacNutt,
'Overcome by the
Spirit' (New Jersey:
Chosen Books, 1984)
pp. 135-8, cited in
Mikhaiel, pp. 35-6.

5. Timothy Hall and
Guy Grant,
'Superpsych'
(Sydney: Methuen,
1976) pp. 26-28.

It is instructive to compare this with the findings of Hall and Grant concerning susceptibility to hypnosis[5]:

> The key to successful hypnosis is motivation.
> The Latin people, the Spanish and the Italians in particular, are usually thought to make better subjects than the less emotional and more suspicious Anglo-Saxons; and near the bottom of any list would be the Teutonic Germans.
> Scientifically minded people generally make rather poor subjects because they are so analytical… Women seem to be more susceptible when they are hypnotised by men…
> There is a clear link between mood and susceptibility, and creativity and susceptibility. Dark moods mean poor subjects, bright moods good subjects; and fantasy and adventure in childhood mean hypnotisability as an adult.

That the Toronto meetings are examples of mass hypnosis is supported by the verdict of five English doctors who attended very similar meetings conducted by John Wimber in the late 80s. Having witnessed the phenomena (trance-like states, trembling, laughing, shaking, falling and so on), all five doctors attributed them to hypnosis. According to one of the five, a leading English psychiatrist, "It was a very expert performance, containing all the textbook characteristics of the induction of hypnosis". (See 'A medical view of miraculous healing', *The Briefing* #33, p. 2).

All this raises serious and important questions, both psychological and theological, which we will return to in a later chapter. We are not accusing Mr Howard-Browne and others of *deliberately* engaging in mass hypnosis, but it seems likely that this is what they are doing, even if unwittingly. They have discovered that if you run a meeting a certain way, and the conditions are right, then certain things happen—strange things, inexplicable things. They have discovered, for example, that it usually takes some time for it all to happen, and readily admit to this. When the strange occurrences finally present themselves, they are then attributed to a powerful and immediate working of God's Spirit.

This is a terrible deception. These occurrences are being sold

to good-hearted Christian believers all over the world as the key
to an ongoing close walk with the Lord, and many are swallowing
the message. We must gently but firmly warn our brothers and
sisters of the danger that they are in. Ultimately, only spiritual
harm will result when we confuse orchestrated hysteria with the
life of true joy and self-control that comes through keeping in
step with the Spirit.

Rodney Howard-Browne is by no means the only face of the Toronto Blessing. Another stream of the movement is represented by Guy (pronounced 'Ghee') Chevreau, who spoke at another recent conference in Sydney.

2 Different streams: same source

GUY CHEVREAU'S BOOK, *Catch the Fire*, is perhaps the best known of the range of publications which attempt to explain and justify what has been happening in the Toronto Blessing.[1] It reveals something of the complex of relationships and influences that has moulded the Toronto movement.

1. G. Chevreau, 'Catch the Fire' (London: Marshall Pickering, 1994).

It seems that the pastor of the Toronto Airport Vineyard, John Arnott, was influenced over a number of years by pentecostal figures such as Kathryn Kulman, Benny Hinn, Rodney Howard-Browne, and Argentinian Assemblies of God head, Claudio Friedzon. It was eventually through the visit of fellow Vineyard pastor Randy Clark (who in turn had been 'set on fire' by Howard-Browne's holy laughter meetings) that the manifestations started to break out in Toronto. It was discovered that the manifestations were transferable, and not only stayed in Toronto after Randy Clark's departure, but spread to other churches whose representatives came to taste 'the anointing'.

Because of these diverse influences and interconnections, it seems that the movement is not a unified one. Some Toronto supporters, for example, while affirming Rodney Howard-Browne's ministry and aware of his role in kicking things off, are a little wary of associating too closely with him (perhaps because of his links to the increasingly discredited Word-Faith movement). Others report being more influenced by the Argentinian branch. Others have more to do with the Toronto Airport Vineyard itself, and its chief apologist Guy Chevreau.

The picture that emerges is of a diverse, somewhat unstructured movement, emanating from the one source. The common denominator is the holding of public meetings where striking physical and emotional phenomena occur which are attributed to the 'manifest presence' of God's Spirit. This diverse unity is reflected in the similarities and differences between the Howard-Browne and Chevreau conferences I attended. In many ways, the differences are embodied in the two men.

Guy Chevreau is something of a Laurel to Rodney Howard-Browne's Hardy. Rodney is short and round, loud and brash; Guy is tall and slim, affable and reflective. Rodney has a certain South African cockiness to his manner, the straight-talking, pugnaciousness of the Afrikaaner; Guy has that easy-going, down-home Canadian charm. Rodney brings with him 15 years of ministry in the pentecostal mainstream; Guy describes himself as a 'recovering Baptist'.

To tall, slim, affable, easy-going chaps like me, Guy Chevreau is certainly the more attractive of the two. At a recent conference, he presented himself as the reasonable face of the movement. According to him, they are not interested in hype or the 'performance' mentality, but in the ongoing fruit of changed lives, of people living in love. They want to keep it simple; they want to stress humility; they want to maintain strong controls over those who are doing the blessing, not allowing excessive touching, and using only same-sex prayer counselling. They want to avoid the 'big leader' syndrome, and consequently have a team of around 30 who do the praying and blessing in their meetings.

All this is commendable. It is what one hopes Christians would do when involved in a phenomenon like this. They would at least try to make sense of it biblically; they would seek to behave rightly and lovingly in the midst of it all; they would try to swing the attention away from themselves.

Nevertheless, in terms of its core beliefs and practices, the Guy Chevreau conference still betrayed its origins in Howard-Browne style pentecostalism. There was the same passion (even necessity) for experiencing the manifest physical presence of God as the key aspect of faith and the Christian life; the same highly

selective use of Scripture and church history to illustrate the va-
lidity of what was taking place; the same confusion between the
hypnotic effects that can be produced by large public meetings
and the work of God's Spirit; the same absence of the cross; and
the same gross distortion of the biblical pattern of Christian life
and service.

Interestingly, in terms of the hypnosis theory, Mr Chevreau
stressed the need to relax if one was to receive the 'blessing', to let
go, to not try to **take** it, but simply to **receive** it (we need to
"unscrunch our foreheads"). There was also talk of the importance of touch in the transfer of the blessing. "There is an element
of physical impartation", he said. Despite the democratization of
praying, it was also stressed that "leadership is key"—the support
and participation of the leaders of a church will ultimately determine whether that particular church tastes the blessing or not.

It was hard not to be drawn to Guy Chevreau's self-effacing,
quietly humorous, gentle manner. But if he represents the reasonable face of the Toronto movement, he is only the more dangerous for doing so.

So far in this booklet, we have looked at the Toronto Blessing as exemplified by Rodney Howard-Browne and Guy Chevreau. We have seen good reasons for being very concerned about the style and direction of what is happening, and suggested that all is by no means well. But along the way, some fairly hefty theological questions have raised their heads and beckoned for attention. It is time we drew back from the details and looked at some of those larger and more basic questions. It is time to consider the shape and emphasis of the thinking that undergirds the Toronto movement.

3 The Toronto Blessing and Real Christianity

IF OUR INITIAL REACTION to the Toronto Blessing is that it seems a world away from New Testament Christianity, we ought to be able to say why. Where have they gone wrong? Or is it that we have gone wrong?

In trying to think biblically about it all, there are at least four very significant questions we need to address:

How does God work in the world?
How do we relate to him?
What is the role of his Spirit?
How do we participate in God's work?

These are all big questions. Each of them on their own could occupy us for many books to come. What is more, they are interconnected. Our answer to one will shape our answer to the others. We will need to paint Rolf Harris-style, with a broad brush, but let us proceed to each of these questions in turn.

How does God act in the world?

What sort of world do we live in? How does God act in his world? How and when should we expect to see him at work? The Toronto Blessing urges these questions upon us, for it claims that God's activity in the world tends to run along quite distinct lines.

For example, when someone falls over with hysterical laughter in a Toronto meeting, this is interpreted as a display of God's power. That God is present and active to bless is displayed by the (seemingly) inexplicable phenomenon that has taken place. However, when the same person does the washing up after the meeting, no-one would interpret this activity in the same way. This would not be seen as a display of God's power in their lives, or an example of God mightily at work. In other words, one sort of activity is a 'spiritual' one, and attributed to God's power; the other is just an ordinary, everyday event.

But why should this be the case? What is there about falling over (or weeping or having deep feelings of 'electricity' or whatever) that is inherently more 'spiritual' than washing up or driving a car or reading a book? Is there a plane of feeling or experience that is more inherently 'spiritual' than another? If we are going to see God at work, should we expect it to be outside the realm of ordinary, everyday things? Does God have a bias towards feelings and strange occurrences? Is that where he tends to operate? Does getting in touch with God mean transcending the ordinary stuff of reality and reaching a higher level of awareness of him?

How, in other words, does God relate to his creation?

The Toronto movement, and pentecostalism generally, would answer that God's action in the world is primarily to be seen in the miraculous, and through powerful, personal encounters with his manifest presence. God may be omnipresent in a general sort of way, but the way he interacts with his world and achieves his purposes is through special intervention. He is to be found in strange, inexplicable and extraordinary experiences—experiences that are without question divine in origin, for they transcend ordinary, everyday, run-of-the-mill reality. If we are to really know him and be blessed by him, we must press beyond the mundane, rational matter of our daily lives to a personal, tangible encounter with him in the realm of 'spirit'.[1]

This way of thinking about how God relates to the world is by no means new to the Toronto Blessing. It has a long ancestry, and might best be described as 'dualism'. We could spend this and many more articles exploring the way that it has affected Christian theology over the centuries and come into the modern mindset. (Those of a philosophical bent can chase up some of that history in Appendix II.)

Dualism makes a profound separation between our 'ordinary' or 'natural' life and the extraordinary or supernatural existence of God. Certain things belong to the 'natural' world (such as science, rational inquiry, objective truths, everyday natural occurrences) and other things belong to the 'supernatural' world (God, spiritual feelings, moral values, faith). There is a gap between these two worlds. There is what Francis Schaeffer called an 'upstairs' and a 'downstairs'. In a dualistic universe, God is seen when he dabbles his fingers in the mechanism of the machine and causes a miracle, or when he intrudes into our everyday personal experience in the arena of intense or 'spiritual' feelings (or when we cross to the 'other side' to experience him).

This way of thinking about God and the world certainly comes very easily to us (thanks to our intellectual history). For the modern person, God is absent from the workaday world. Those who wish to find him search for a sign that he is really there, some point of contact. They want him to show himself in some way in a demonstration of his power. God is sought in the arena of miracle and personal mystical encounter.

It is this sort of assumption about God and the way he relates to the world that lies behind the pentecostal emphasis on subjective feeling and miracles. God is sought in the strange and the extraordinary. We get in touch with him when we feel him, when his 'manifest presence' is in our meeting to bless us. This is the 'spiritual' sector. It is where the action is, as far as God is concerned.

When we turn to the Bible we see a very different picture of God and his creation. In love, God creates a world that is separate from himself, that is an independent, existing thing. Yet, he remains sovereign over his creation, and is constantly present to it. He is not absent. He is always active in the world, in both the ordinary and extraordinary. There is no 'upstairs' and 'downstairs'. There is no God-of-the-gaps spirituality, where God shows that he still exists by intruding into our normal, rational, everyday lives in miracles and mystical experiences.

1. Chevreau's 'Catch the Fire' exemplifies this approach (see especially chapter 3). Some representative quotes: "It is the **experiential** reality of God that stands at the centre of biblical faith" (emphasis his, p. 41); "Throughout the history of the Church, it has been the experience of God's 'felt' presence that has called men and women to faith and to mission" (p. 44); "We began with a brief consideration of God's **omnispresence**; the focus of our attention now is the **manifest** presence of God. Not propositional belief, the substance of faith, but personal **experience**, whereby we personally, hear and feel the immediate nearness of God" (emphasis his, p. 45).

All things considered

Are not two sparrows sold for a penny? Yet not one of them will fall to the ground apart from the will of your Father. (Matt 10:29).

By the word of the LORD were the heavens made, their starry host by the breath of his mouth. (Ps 33:6).

The Son is the radiance of God's glory and the exact representation of his being, sustaining all things by his powerful word. (Heb 1:3).

But he said to me, "My grace is sufficient for you, for my power is made perfect in weakness." Therefore I will boast all the more gladly about my weaknesses, so that Christ's power may rest on me. (2 Cor 12:9).

According to the Scriptures, the Living God is at work in all his creation—in the fall of the sparrow and in the resurrection of Christ from the dead (Matt 10:29*, cf. Eph 1:17-23). Just as he created all things by his Word, by the Spirit/Breath of his mouth (Gen 1; Ps 33:6*), so he still upholds all things by his powerful Word (Col 1:17; Heb 1:3*). When we see the sun doing its circuit like a champion athlete running his course, we should praise the wondrous power and wisdom of God at work (Ps 19:1-6; cf. Rom 1:18f.).

Indeed, perhaps the very categories of 'natural' and 'supernatural' concede too much to a dualistic way of thinking about God in the world. It is not as if some things take place outside his activity and others not. He works in and through his own creation to achieve his purposes. Creation is putty in his hands. He gives it a certain shape, and it tends to follow certain regular patterns as he establishes and upholds them, but the putty remains quite malleable as far as he is concerned (even if it seems hard and regular to us). He can work with it and shape it as he wills. We need to perceive, as G. K. Chesterton put it, the magic that is everywhere in creation, the dance of the molecules, with God himself behind and in it all, conducting the orchestra.

Following on from this, there is no conception in the Bible's view of creation that God operates more in the area of feelings or extraordinary experiences than in any other. Our emotions are as much his creation as are our minds. Our feelings are not a special contact point with God where we truly do business with him. We are whole persons, created in God's image, and he deals with us as such. In our Christian lives there will be times of great happiness, excitement and emotional release, just as there will periods of sadness, suffering, pain, and persecution, not to mention other periods of hard, tedious, endurance. There will be a whole range of experience, and we should not think that God is to be found more in one aspect or emotional state, than another.

Indeed, it is interesting to reflect on the strand of biblical teaching that sees God's power and presence especially manifest in weakness (2 Cor 12:9*). In the proclamation of what the world regards as a pathetically ordinary message about a crucified man, the very wisdom and power of God is shown, a wisdom and

26

power that is only discerned by the spiritual (1 Cor 1:18-2:16*).

When God relates to his creation—when he relates to *us*—he doesn't zap us from outside in some trans-dimensional way. He is committed to his creation and works in and through it, with all its gritty and grubby realities—as both the Incarnation and the Cross show. He achieves his purposes according to 'nature' (or should we say 'the created order'). He is quite free to interrupt the regularities of the created order as it suits him, and it remains malleable to him to direct as he pleases. But we must not set up a dualism whereby we focus on the extraordinary and the emotional, as if feelings and the extraordinary are God's special domain. To do so is to distort the biblical doctrine of creation.

> Jews demand miraculous signs and Greeks look for wisdom, but we preach Christ crucified: a stumbling-block to Jews and foolishness to Gentiles, but to those whom God has called, both Jews and Greeks, Christ the power of God and the wisdom of God. (1 Cor 1:22-24).

How do we relate to him?

All theology is interconnected. One area of thought will always have some bearing on another. In this case, what we believe about how God works in the world will determine to a large extent how we are to relate to him. Our doctrine of creation will flow through into our gospel.

If we believe, for example, that God's activity in the world is to be seen primarily in the arena of miracles and intense personal experience, then how we relate to him will obviously focus on that area. The emphasis will be on satisfying our thirst for God by drinking from the fountain, by catching the fire, by soaking in the blessing, by walking in the anointing (all phrases used at Toronto meetings I have attended). The call will be, "Come and experience it for yourself. Yield to God and trust that he is ready to bless you in this way."

This tangible nearness of God's presence becomes the stuff of our relationship with God. It will be the assurance that we are in touch with him. It will energize our daily walk. It will embolden us for witness. It will motivate us to holiness. It will be the attraction to draw in outsiders (that in this place we are in touch with the manifest presence of the living God). It becomes the essence of Christian life and ministry. It becomes, in other words, our gospel.

God demonstrates his own love for us in this: While we were still sinners, Christ died for us...When we were God's enemies, we were reconciled to him through the death of his Son... (Rom 5:8,10).

We have renounced secret and shameful ways; we do not use deception, nor do we distort the word of God. On the contrary, by setting forth the truth plainly we commend ourselves to every man's conscience in the sight of God. (2 Cor 4:2).

Since, then, you have been raised with Christ, set your hearts on things above, where Christ is seated at the right hand of God. Set your minds on things above, not on earthly things. For you died, and your life is now hidden with Christ in God. When Christ, who is your life, appears, then you also will appear with him in glory. (Col 3:1-4).

This is the good news that the Toronto Blessing proclaims—that if you are 'dry' then here is a way to relate to God that will satisfy your thirst. If you are distant from him, there is a way to get close. This is built on the assumption, we must remember, that the place to truly encounter God is on the plane of feelings and miraculous activity.

However, if we start with a biblical view of creation (as above) the basic problem we face in relating to God is not being trapped in the 'physical', rational world. It is not as if he is 'upstairs' and our problem is being stuck 'downstairs'. Nor is our problem a lack of spiritual feeling, as if that were the area in which he is primarily to be found, and we have not found him.

Our real problem is the separation in relationship from God because of sin. The difficulty facing us is not breaking through or rising above the normal stuff of creation so as to experience the Spirit. The difficulty is our rebellion. The face-to-face fellowship of Eden has been broken through our enmity with God. The creation needs reconciling to its Creator, and this is something we are powerless to do ourselves.

Thus the creator himself takes the initiative, enters his creation in the person of his Son, Jesus Christ, and dies for its redemption. The 'weak and foolish' cross of Christ is God's power and wisdom, through which those who once were enemies are now reconciled (Rom 5:6-10★). Just as he created the world through a word, so also he creates new life in us through a word, through the ordinary things of his created order—words being preached by created persons about a man dying on a cross (2 Cor 4:1-6★; 1 Pet 1:23). Words are the way persons relate. When God solves our basic problem—the fractured relationship with him—he does so by speaking to us.

In other words, we relate to God through the gospel—not just at the beginning of our Christian lives but always. Through our union by faith with Christ in his death and resurrection, we are raised up to sit with him at God's side (Rom 6:1f; Eph 2:1-10; Col 3:1-4). One day, our union with him will be fully manifest and we will see him face to face. In the meantime, our life in Christ is a hidden life (Col 3:1-4★); we live by faith, not by sight (Rom 8:24-25). To seek the full manifestation now is an error in

28

eschatology (that is, mistaking what will be ours in heaven with what is ours now).

In Christ is all the fullness of God, and since we are in him through the gospel, we also have received fullness (Col 2:6-3:4). This is the reality for those who have repented and put their faith in Christ. The Scriptures say very little about what it feels like, for it is not primarily a matter of feeling—as if our basic problem is being separated from feeling God. The problem is a broken relationship, and in Christ that relationship is reconciled.

The role of the Spirit

How the Holy Spirit fits into all this flows from how God works in the world and how we relate to him through the gospel.

If God is to be contacted chiefly in the arena of personal experience and the miraculous, then the Spirit will be the mediator of that experience to us. The Spirit will be the one who 'bridges the gap', who allows us to feel God's manifest presence in the room, and to do business with him. This has been the historic emphasis of pentecostalism—that the Spirit is the neglected member of the Trinity who brings us back into contact with a 'real' experience of God, through feeling his presence and participating in miraculous gifts. The Toronto Blessing is an undiluted example of this way of thinking about the Spirit.

However, if God works in and through all the created order, not simply or especially in the arena of feelings, and if his purposes involve reconciling persons to himself through the gospel of Christ crucified, then this too will be the role of the Spirit. It is not as if the work of the Spirit is separate or tangential in some way to all this. The Lord is the Spirit (2 Cor 3:17). He is active in the world, working in and through the creation to achieve his purposes. The Spirit's work is the same as that of the Son, which is the Father's work also (see John 14-16).

And so, as the word of the gospel is proclaimed, the Spirit wields it as his own sword (Eph 6:17*) and creates new life in us, washing us and renewing us (Tit 3:5-7*), bringing the Father and Son to make their home with us (Jn 14:15-23), guaranteeing us our inheritance in the eternal kingdom (Eph 1:13-14), produc-

Take the helmet of salvation and the sword of the Spirit, which is the word of God. (Eph 6:17).

He saved us, not because of righteous things we had done, but because of his mercy. He saved us through the washing of rebirth and renewal by the Holy Spirit, whom he poured out on us generously through Jesus Christ our Saviour, so that, having been justified by his grace, we might become heirs having the hope of eternal life. (Tit 3:5-7).

All things considered

ing in us the fruit of Christlike character as we await that inherit-ance (Rom 8:9-17; Gal 5:16-26), and empowering us to build up others to that same end (1 Cor 12-14).

In other words, the Spirit's work focuses on the restoration of our relationship with God; he is the Spirit of sonship, leading us to cry 'Abba, Father'. Since God's purposes are to transform us as whole persons into the image of his Son, it should not surprise us that the Spirit's ongoing work in the Christian life centres around leading us to put to death the misdeeds of the body, and produce the fruit of a changed life amidst all our difficulties and struggles (Rom 8:9-17). This is why self-control, rather than self-abandon or loss of control, is a mark of the Spirit's powerful presence (Gal 5:22-23★; also see 2 Tim 1:7-8★).

This, then, is what the Triune God is doing in us, and in our world. The remarkable thing is that we have a part to play in this work, not only as joyful recipients of its benefits, but as God's fellow-workers.

> But the fruit of the Spirit is love, joy, peace, patience, kindness, goodness, faithfulness, gentleness and self-control. Against such things there is no law. (Gal 5:22-23).

> For God did not give us a spirit of timidity, but a spirit of power, of love and of self-discipline. So do not be ashamed to testify about our Lord, or ashamed of me his prisoner. But join with me in suffering for the gospel, by the power of God, (2 Tim 1:7-8).

Our participation in God's work

If this is the nature of creation, the gospel and the Spirit, what will *our* part in God's work look like? In other words, what will ministry be like?

Again, it will flow out of our doctrines of creation and salva-tion, for the gospel contains our task within it. We have been reconciled to God through the word of the cross, and our task is to be ministers of reconciliation to others (2 Cor 5:14-21). God works through his creation (by humans speaking to other hu-mans) to do his work. As Martin Luther saw so clearly, the cross is not simply an event; it is also the revelation of our gospel, the shape of our theology and the nature of our ministry. In suffering and weakness, and in the plain setting forth of the Word of truth by people as ordinary as jars of clay, God works mightily by his Spirit to open blind eyes, to create light where there was darkness (2 Cor 4:1-18).

When we glance through the New Testament, time and again this is what our role in God's work is like. It is a ministry built around the word of the gospel, preached and lived; a ministry preoccupied with Christ crucified, both as the content and manner of what is done; a ministry conducted with sincerity, intelligibility and good order, with a loving involvement in the lives of our hearers. It is built on prayer, and the preaching and teaching of the Word in season and out, warning and encouraging everyone to frame their lives by this sound doctrine. You might want to phrase it differently or add a few bits and pieces, but this is the sort of picture you would get from the New Testament.

That Toronto-style ministry looks very different from this should not surprise us, given what we have seen so far. If God is to be found and related to in personal mystical encounter and through extraordinary happenings, then ministry will focus on events at which these encounters take place. The life-blood of the Toronto movement, and of pentecostalism generally, is the meeting (large or small) at which the personal touch of God is experienced by the individual. Our part in God's work at one level will simply be to yield to him and experience the blessing; at another level, we will try to spread the experience to others, running meetings and praying for others so that they might also catch the fire.

Conclusion

By standing back and looking at some of the broader biblical issues that are at stake in the Toronto debate, we have begun to see why an initial reaction of uneasiness and caution is justified. It is not simply that a few extreme or hysterical things take place—although they clearly do. The real problem is deeper and more fundamental.

The Toronto movement rests on faulty ideas about how God works in the world and how we basically relate to him. When these ideas filter through to views about God's Spirit and what Christian life and ministry ought to be like, we end up with a picture far different from the one we find in the Scriptures.

Here, as far as I can see, lies the real danger inherent in the Toronto Blessing and other pentecostal movements of its type. By offering a means of relating to God, being blessed by him, and getting close to him, that is quite apart from or beyond the biblical gospel of Christ, they distract us from that gospel. They construct an alternative Christianity.

This is a hard thing to say, but given what we have seen thus far, can we avoid saying it? Certainly, many of those involved are good Christian people, who would affirm their belief in Jesus' death for their sins and the need to preach the gospel—even if in their practice they move beyond these things. Not everything they do will be wrong. Depending on the biblical maturity and godliness of those involved, there will be a range of belief and practice, with some being more faithful to the Bible than others. And God will doubtless work some good out of it in his sovereign way.

All the same, when we see brothers and sisters wandering away from the truth, we ought to speak the truth in love. We need to tell them that Toronto-style Christianity is not biblical Christianity. It has different basic assumptions about how God works in the world, how we relate to him, what his Spirit does and what our lives and ministries should be like. It moves in a different direction, and calls upon other Christians to follow.

In doing so it is being faithless, for God has given us a gospel and commanded us to guard it and to preach it. We are not to preach an alternative way of relating to him, nor add anything to the gospel he has given us. He has given us a job to do, a message to deliver, and we must discharge this duty faithfully, in the face of everpresent alternatives. If we find ourselves moving beyond this or being distracted into something different, we must come to our senses and renew our grasp on the truth.

Watch your life and doctrine closely. Persevere in them, because if you do, you will save both yourself and your hearers. (1 Tim 4:16).

The opportunities for pressing forward together in the work God has given us to do are enormous and exciting. Let us harness our energies to *this* end, knowing that if we watch our life and doctrine closely, we will save both ourselves and our hearers (1 Tim 4:16★).

The rather negative assessment I have made of the Toronto Blessing has been challenged at a number of points. It is worth dealing with some of those objections here, if only briefly.

4 | Objections

What about the fruit?

Some object that this new movement must be from God, since it is producing so much 'fruit'. They point to the churches and individuals who have been given a new lease of life by participating in the Toronto Blessing. Surely the presence of such fruit indicates that the movement is genuine.

Firstly, it would be hard to think of any Christian movement, no matter how bad, from which no good has come. With a sovereign God, good will come even come out of evil.

In this case, it is hardly surprising that people are feeling enthused and invigorated by their participation in the experience, whether it is from God or not. The emotional impact of what is happening is considerable. Deep emotional wells are being tapped, and people are feeling cleansed and released from pent-up fears and inhibitions. There is no doubting the fact that a good long laugh is very therapeutic. On top of this, numbers may well be up at the church as people come to see what is happening.

What's more, if those involved fervently believe that all this is a result of being touched by God's Spirit—whether it really is or not—the effect is only magnified. They will feel even more enthused, emboldened and invigorated, since the experience is attributed to God's special intervention. It is very possible, in other words, that much of the so-called 'fruit' associated with the Toronto Blessing is something of a spiritual placebo effect.[1]

The question is: Does any of this tell us what God wants us to be doing? Should we start with someone who has been encouraged or boosted along in some way, and argue back from there

1. For those not familiar with the term, a placebo is a medicine which performs no physiological function (like a sugar pill) but which improves the patient's health through his belief that it really is a powerful medicine.

that whatever helped them is God's new method of refreshing his church? Should we cast around for some methodology that people find invigorating and exciting and conclude, *ipso facto*, that this should be the focus of Christian ministry? As Paul argues so forcefully in the first eight verses of Romans 3, ends don't justify means. We should start with what God has told us to be doing (in the New Testament) and get on with it.

Only in large meetings?

Some also question the suggestion that a large 'hyped' meeting is necessary for the Toronto experiences to occur. They report that similar things have happened on much smaller, more low-key occasions.

It wasn't suggested in chapter 1 (on Rodney Howard-Browne) that all the hype of a large, emotionally manipulative meeting is a prerequisite for such phenomena to occur. Elements such as motivation to participate, expectation of outcome, leadership towards that outcome, group reinforcement, and imitation of others so affected, can also be present in smaller meetings. This may well explain the phenomena occurring in those contexts. It is also significant, I think, that outbreaks of Toronto-style phenomena only seem to occur by transfer—someone from a 'Toronto' church takes the 'blessing' to another church before the manifestations occur. The element of auto-suggestive imitation still seems to be present, even in smaller, less extreme contexts.

The more serious question underlying this, however, is the one addressed in chapter 3. Why is it that certain abnormal events are to be investigated as possible 'spiritual manifestations' whereas other more normal activities are not? I won't repeat the argument here.

Do feelings have no place then?

Some might respond to what I have written by asking: Does that mean that there is no place for emotions in the Christian life? Should our Christian experience be like one long dull sermon, filled with words but no passion?

Even phrasing the question in that way indicates that the answer must be: Of course not! We are whole people, created by God with emotions, and our relationship with God will call forth a whole variety of emotional responses. There will be times of intense happiness and exhilaration; and others of intense sorrow (cf. 2 Cor 7:8-11*); and still others of quiet, patient perseverance. The Christian life will encompass a whole gamut of emotions, called forth as we seek to live out our new relationship with God in the midst of a sinful world.

However, this does not mean that our emotions are the particular place where we do business with God, as I argued in chapter 3. We must not equate emotion with 'spirituality'. We relate to God through faith in Jesus, and this will have a variety of emotional effects, depending on the situations we are in, and the kind of people we are. We should not hide from our emotions, as if they were inappropriate or unseemly; nor should we seek particular emotional experiences, as if they were the essence of real relationship with God.

If there is one emotion we should actively cultivate, according to the New Testament, it is joy. But even this is as much an action as an emotion; it is something we are commanded to do, even in the most difficult of circumstances (cf. 2 Cor 6:3-10; Jas 1:2*).

Even if I caused you sorrow by my letter, I do not regret it. Though I did regret it—I see that my letter hurt you, but only for a little while—yet now I am happy, not because you were made sorry, but because your sorrow led you to repentance. For you became sorrowful as God intended and so were not harmed in any way by us. Godly sorrow brings repentance that leads to salvation and leaves no regret, but worldly sorrow brings death. (2 Cor 7:8-10).

Consider it pure joy, my brothers, whenever you face trials of many kinds, (Jas 1:2).

Among the numerous stories in the secular media about the Toronto Blessing, one was of particular interest. Journalist Mick Brown attended the 'Catch the Fire' convention in Toronto, in October 1994, and wrote up his experience in the Telegraph Magazine *(Daily Telegraph, London, Saturday December 3, 1994). His article 'Unzipper Heaven, Lord. Ha-ha, ho-ho, he-he…' has reputedly become one of the most widely-read articles on Toronto in the secular press.*

He-he isn't Lord

MICK BROWN IS INTERESTED in strange phenomena and religious experience. He is not a Christian and did not go to the conference intending to become one. The interesting thing is, he experienced the full blessing. In his article he wrote, "I found myself beside John Arnott...I didn't even see his hand coming as it arced through the air and touched me gently—hardly at all—on the forehead...I could feel a palpable shock running through me, then I was falling backwards, as if my legs had been kicked away from underneath me.

"I hit the floor—I swear this is the truth—laughing like a drain."

Mick Brown is the sort of person who might be called an 'open-minded inquirer'. "I'm not and I wasn't a practising Christian before going to Toronto", he says, "but I've always had an interest in all sorts of different religious experience, the phenomena of religious experience—just the notion of a quest for the meaning of life, more than just the four corners of the materialistic world." He approached the meeting in a somewhat sceptical manner. "I hadn't bargained for the experience before I went, and, in fact, the more time I spent there, the more reluctant I became of partaking in it personally. The reason was that, nice as the people were that I met, charming and accommodating, friendly and loving as they were towards me and the photographer, there are aspects of that sort of evangelical Christianity which I don't particularly buy into, and don't particularly like. For instance, the aspect of the kind of political conservatism that often comes along with it, and the sense of a very rigid, rather dogmatic worldview, and the idea that knowledge of God or religious experience is somehow the exclusive prerogative of the Christian religion. And I don't believe that myself.

"I think that every culture and every faith expresses an understanding of God or the divine, in their own particular way, and the divine does not discriminate between different cultures, between different religions."

What Christians want to know, of course, is what effect this experience had on him. Any reputed work of the Spirit is to be judged by its fruit; we are told by the spokespeople for the Toronto Blessing that this is something which will renew Christ's church. Did any such renewing work of the Spirit happen in Mick Brown's life? He states that he has never experienced long-term consequences from any other religious experience, "nor did I have any long-term consequence from the 'Toronto blessing'. What happened was that I fell down laughing, as I described, and was on the floor for about ten minutes. I got up rather dazed but perfectly happy and relaxed.

"What I didn't say in that article was that what happened next was that Pastor John Arnott's wife came over and said: 'Can I bless you again?' And she put her hand on my forehead (with my own consent this time), and I fell back again—but not laughing that time. I was probably too exhausted; it was then one o'clock in the morning and I had been on my feet since eight the previous morning. But I felt very relaxed and very happy.

"People knelt down beside me in a generous spirit and started to pray over me. I became slightly worried, and started to feel a sort of obligational responsibility to them, as if I ought to suddenly spring up and say that I had found Christ. I didn't do that, and I don't know if they were disappointed because I didn't. But that's just the kind of social pressure that that kind of situation brings to bear on one.

"Nor did I feel any kind of longer term effects. I spoke to various people who were at that particular conference, who had the experience before, and were prepared to testify that it had reinforced their faith, their belief in Christ. It made them, in a way, more dutiful Christians. They had returned to their Bible studies with a greater appetite. It had confirmed them in their faith—that was the main thing—they were in no doubt that this was a blessing of God, a blessing of the Holy Spirit.

"I didn't feel I had their faith to be confirmed in. It didn't change in any way my reservations about fundamental Christianity, you know, this purchase on God. It didn't make me think that Buddhism, Hinduism, Islam, Red Indian Shamanism or whatever other kind of manifestation of faith could go out with the bathwater."

Mick Brown believed in God before he had the experience, but it was not the Christian God. "I'm sure (like most people) I don't have a very clear idea of the kind of God I believe in. I think that one of the things I find most attractive about Eastern philosophy, about Buddhist philosophy is that it doesn't propose a separateness between man and the divine. But it actually supposes that man awakens to the fact of divinity within himself. But I do believe in an active force or energy, or whatever, that is the animating force of all life. I believe it is essentially benign, and that it is us who cloud the benign aspect through our own egos, our grasp of power and possessions, through vanity, ambition and all the attachments we surround ourselves with, that we strive for."

Brown's view of God was not changed by the experience. Neither was his view of Jesus. "Well, I have no doubts about the historic existence of Christ. I used to have a childlike, unquestioning acceptance of the Bible stories, Sunday school, gentle Jesus, the manifestation of good, the Son of God and so on. [Brown attended a Methodist Sunday School.] I think that perhaps now I would say that Christ was a sort of man, someone through whom God was working. Certainly, that's my understanding, my interpretation, of someone who was an 'enlightened' being. I've always tried to make a very strong distinction between the truth at the heart of any religion and the dogma that grows around it. So whatever reservations I might have about fundamental Christianity, are not reservations I would have about Christ, or whatever I believe Christ to be." He says that this view has not changed since Toronto.

Mick Brown is by his own admission not a Christian, and his stated beliefs about God and Christ bear that out. This was the

case both before and after experiencing the blessing which is sup-
posed to be from God's Spirit, whose work (the Bible tells us) is
to point to Christ and bring people to Christ-likeness. Mick Brown
clearly testifies that in his case, the Toronto Blessing did no such
thing.

(Based on an interview in *Evangelicals Now*, February 1995.
Adapted, with permission, by Kirsty Birkett.)

A little more about Dualism

IN CHAPTER 3, we referred to the way of viewing God and the world that is known as 'dualism'.

Dualism goes back, at the most basic level, to Plato, with his chasm between the perfect Ideals of the other world, and the grubby matter of this world. It has percolated down via Greek philosophy into a variety of Christian and sub-Christian theologies. It lay behind the world-denying Gnosticism of the 2nd century, and exercised particular influence in the middle ages. It has given rise to mysticism in all its different forms, which attempts to escape the hindrances and distractions of physical creation and cross the gap to the 'spiritual' God on the other side.

Most interestingly, this dualistic way of thinking has also figured prominently in modern thought. The Deists of the 18th and 19th centuries, for example, saw God as the cosmic Watchmaker who created the intricate mechanism of the world according to certain immutable laws, wound it up, and left it to run. For the Deist, God is the Creator, but has no ongoing involvement in the running of the world. The world proceeds by the 'natural' principles which God built into the mechanism.

The philosophy of Immanuel Kant (1724-1804), which has had such a momentous influence on modern thought, also contains this profound dualism between the unknowable Other, and the world we know and experience through our senses. For Kant, all religion and metaphysics belongs to the 'other' world (the 'noumenal' as he called it), and is unknown to us and unavailable to the rational mind. Friedrich Schleiermacher (1768-1834) built a whole theology on this assumption, one which has also been massively influential in our own century. He agreed with Kant that God was not knowable rationally, but asserted that this was not the end of the story—God could still be experienced in the realm of feeling.

Much contemporary thought about God and religion drifts along the currents of thought that flow from Kant and Schleiermacher—the idea that 'God' and 'religion' are entirely subjective and matters of feeling, that the world operates according to inbuilt principles without God's activity, the radical distinction between 'facts' and 'values', the view that sees faith as a blind leap into the rationally unknowable and unprovable, and so on.

Assumptions like these about the world, and God's relation to it, also lie behind pentecostalism and the Toronto Blessing. In this sense, it is a very modern movement, even if its ancestry goes back a long way.